SPORTS GREAT MUGGSY BOGUES

—Sports Great Books—

BASEBALL

Sports Great Jim Abbott
0-89490-395-0/ Savage

Sports Great Barry Bonds
0-89490-595-3/ Sullivan

Sports Great Bobby Bonilla
0-89490-417-5/ Knapp

Sports Great Roger Clemens
0-89490-284-9/ Devaney

Sports Great Orel Hershiser
0-89490-389-6/ Knapp

Sports Great Bo Jackson
0-89490-281-4/ Knapp

Sports Great Greg Maddux
0-89490-873-1/ Thornley

Sports Great Kirby Puckett
0-89490-392-6/ Aaseng

Sports Great Cal Ripken, Jr.
0-89490-387-X/ Macnow

Sports Great Nolan Ryan
0-89490-394-2/ Lace

Sports Great Darryl Strawberry
0-89490-291-1/ Torres & Sullivan

BASKETBALL

Sports Great Charles Barkley
0-89490-386-1/ Macnow

Sports Great Larry Bird
0-89490-368-3/ Kavanagh

Sports Great Muggsy Bogues
0-89490-876-6/ Rekela

Sports Great Patrick Ewing
0-89490-369-1/ Kavanagh

Sports Great Anfernee Hardaway
0-89490-758-1/ Rekela

**Sports Great Magic Johnson
(Revised and Expanded)**
0-89490-348-9/ Haskins

Sports Great Michael Jordan
0-89490-370-5/ Aaseng

Sports Great Karl Malone
0-89490-599-6/ Savage

Sports Great Reggie Miller
0-89490-874-X/ Thornley

Sports Great Alonzo Mourning
0-89490-875-8/ Fortunato

Sports Great Hakeem Olajuwon
0-89490-372-1/ Knapp

Sports Great Shaquille O'Neal
0-89490-594-5/ Sullivan

Sports Great Scottie Pippen
0-89490-755-7/ Bjarkman

Sports Great David Robinson
0-89490-373-X/ Aaseng

Sports Great Dennis Rodman
0-89490-759-X/ Thornley

Sports Great John Stockton
0-89490-598-8/ Aaseng

Sports Great Isiah Thomas
0-89490-374-8/ Knapp

Sports Great Dominique Wilkins
0-89490-754-9/ Bjarkman

FOOTBALL

Sports Great Troy Aikman
0-89490-593-7/ Macnow

Sports Great John Elway
0-89490-282-2/ Fox

Sports Great Jim Kelly
0-89490-670-4/ Harrington

Sports Great Joe Montana
0-89490-371-3/ Kavanagh

Sports Great Jerry Rice
0-89490-419-1/ Dickey

Sports Great Barry Sanders
0-89490-418-3/ Knapp

Sports Great Herschel Walker
0-89490-207-5/ Benagh

HOCKEY

Sports Great Wayne Gretzky
0-89490-757-3/ Rappoport

Sports Great Mario Lemieux
0-89490-596-1/ Knapp

TENNIS

Sports Great Steffi Graf
0-89490-597-X/ Knapp

Sports Great Pete Sampras
0-89490-756-5/ Sherrow

SPORTS GREAT MUGGSY BOGUES

George Rekela

—Sports Great Books—

Enslow Publishers, Inc.

44 Fadem Road	PO Box 38
Box 699	Aldershot
Springfield, NJ 07081	Hants GU12 6BP
USA	UK

Library of Congress Cataloging-in-Publication Data

Rekela, George R., 1943–
    Sports great Muggsy Bogues / George Rekela.
        p. cm. — (Sports great books)
    Includes index.
    Summary: Looks at the life story, including the college and professional
basketball careers, of Charlotte Hornets star Tyrone Bogues.
    ISBN 0-89490-876-6
    1. Bogues, Tyrone, 1965– —Juvenile literature. 2. Basketball players—United
States—Biography—Juvenile literature. [1. Bogues, Tyrone, 1965– . 2. Basketball
players. 3. Afro-Americans—Biography.] I. Title. II. Series.
GV884.B64R45   1997   96-14170
796.323'092—dc20   CIP
[B]   AC

Printed in the United States of America

10 9 8 7 6 5 4 3 2 1

Photo Credits: Brian Drake/Sports Chrome East/West, pp. 8, 11, 12, 15, 18, 21,
42, 45, 48, 55, 59, 60; Roger W. Winstead, Wake Forest University, p. 36; Wake
Forest University, pp. 25, 27, 30, 32, 38.

Cover Photo: Brian Drake/Sports Chrome East/West

Contents

Chapter 1

Six-foot-seven-inch, 250-pound Anthony Mason of the New York Knicks grabbed the ball and took off down the floor headed for an easy slam-dunk basket and a four-point overtime lead over the Charlotte Hornets. Seemingly from out of nowhere came the Charlotte Hornets' five-foot-three-inch, 136-pound Tyrone "Muggsy" Bogues. Mason didn't even realize he was in a footrace. Perhaps if he had, he might have won.

The streaking Bogues made up the distance of half the court to catch Mason just past the foul line. The other eight players on the floor appeared to be moving toward them in a slow-motion ballet.

New York and Charlotte were well into their second overtime of the evening in the third game of the best-of-seven 1993 National Basketball Association Eastern Conference semifinals. The Knicks had taken a 106–104 lead with two minutes and twenty-four seconds left. A basket by Mason would have made it 108–104, but it never happened.

Muggsy Bogues's small size helped him to launch a surprise attack against Anthony Mason of the New York Knicks in the 1993 Eastern Conference semifinals.

Amazingly, Bogues caught up with Mason and slapped at the ball, altering its course. The ball bounced off of Mason and flew out of bounds.

The play had started with the Hornets on offense. Charlotte's Johnny Newman had attempted to go around Mason. For no apparent reason, Newman lost his balance. The ball landed at Mason's feet, and he was off to the races.

"At first," Bogues subsequently recalled, "I thought John was going to recover, so I didn't move. Then I just tried to run Mason down. I thought I could foul him." Then fate played a hand. Mason, who had been dribbling with his right hand, abruptly switched to his left. This was all Bogues needed to reach the ball. When it landed out of bounds, two minutes and twelve seconds remained in the overtime period.

The game was incredibly close, as the Knicks and Hornets had been less than four points apart ever since three minutes remained in regulation time. A basket by Mason would have put New York safely in the lead on their way to a 3–0 advantage in the series.

But the game was not over yet. Players from both the Knicks and the Hornets had been pushed to the limit. Forty-eight minutes of regulation play plus a fifteen minute overtime period had sapped their energy, but failed to produce an outcome. The first overtime had ended with the score tied at 102.

Now it was the second overtime. After Bogues slapped the ball away from Mason, Charlotte tied the score. It was the eighteenth time during the course of this incredible game that a tie score had been reached. Then, with less than a minute left in the period, the Knicks missed a shot, and with it, their opportunity to take the lead. The Hornets gained possession.

Bogues, by far the shortest player on the floor, dribbled the ball up the floor and eyed the Knicks defense. Suddenly,

Bogues raised his fist, then whipped the ball to teammate Kendall Gill. Gill instantly realized what Bogues was up to. It was the old "give and go" play where a player passes to another, breaks toward the basket, and receives a return pass. Gill passed to the driving Bogues, who fired a jump shot at the basket and hit nothing but net. Charlotte had the lead, 108–106. Fifty-three seconds remained in the second overtime period.

"I wasn't hesitant," said Bogues as he remembered the shot. "I was looking for my shot, and the shot felt good. The worst thing you can do is miss. I hit some big shots, and I've got to keep taking them."

New York called for a time-out. Coach Pat Riley drew up a play setting up the Knicks' seven-foot all-pro center Patrick Ewing. When play resumed, the Knicks passed the ball around the perimeter then went to Ewing. He missed a twelve-foot jump shot over Hornets' center Alonzo Mourning. The ball clanged off the back of the rim and headed toward the sidelines. Charlotte's David Wingate and New York's Charles Oakley gave chase. Both players grabbed at the ball and touched it as it went out of bounds. Referee Ronnie Nunn ruled that Oakley had touched it last. Thirty-four seconds remained and Charlotte would have the ball.

Now it was Charlotte coach Allan Bristow's turn to call a time-out. Bristow called for a play that would drain twenty seconds off the clock, then have Mourning take the shot. Floor leader Bogues took the inbounds pass and dribbled the ball back and forth as the clock ticked away. Mourning worked his way free, and Bogues hit him with a pass. Mourning missed a fourteen-foot shot. Oakley and Mason lunged for the rebound, but knocked each other off the ball, which landed out of bounds. It was Charlotte's ball and twelve seconds showed on the clock.

Bogues took the inbounds pass and immediately was

fouled by Hubert Davis. There were no free throws for the foul, so Charlotte had to take the ball out again. What happened next was an instant replay of the previous play. Davis fouled Bogues. But this time, New York was over the foul limit, and Bogues went to the foul line. The second foul happened with five seconds left.

Bogues calmly bounced the ball before his foul shot. He was brimming with confidence. There was no way he would miss. The shot left his hand and settled in the basket, 109–106 Charlotte. Another free throw would cinch victory. Without hesitation, he arched his second shot toward the basket. It dropped through. The Knicks' John Starks missed a desperation shot, and the Hornets celebrated their victory.

"That was a tough, tough loss for us, and a great win for

Eyeing the defense, Bogues drives up the lane.

Muggsy Bogues celebrates with Alonzo Mourning after the win.

them," coach Riley told observers in the Knicks' locker room. "We've got to understand that we're in a very competitive series here. You have got to give the Hornets a lot of credit."

Most of the credit went to Muggsy Bogues, the smallest player on the floor, who had scored 16 points and dished out 8 assists.

"Muggsy's lightning out there," said teammate Larry Johnson, recalling Bogues's steal of the ball from Mason. "Speed and heart. That's what he is all about."

Back in the Knicks' locker room, Starks was talking to reporters and marveling about a play very late in the first overtime. New York had cleared the lane to set him up at the top of the key against Bogues. Starks is fourteen inches taller than Bogues, so it appeared to be a serious mismatch. Starks methodically backed down his man until only four seconds remained. He then obeyed some inner signal, hesitated, and brought the ball forward. The quicker Bogues reached in and batted it away. Starks thought he had been fouled. In the Charlotte dressing room, Bogues was asked about the play. "There was no foul," he said. "He brought the ball right to me," Bogues said with a smile.

Chapter 2

You are only limited by the size of your dreams.

Ten years ago, National Basketball Association experts would have told you that it was impossible for a player to make it in the league and be only five feet three inches tall. In those days, most would have said that any players measuring under six feet were doomed before the first tip-off. The NBA in the mid-1980s was becoming a league of giants. Six-foot-six-inch point guards were common.

Then along came a man who fooled all the experts. Against monumental odds, Tyrone Bogues astounded people with his tough style of play. His is one of the greatest stories in the history of sports.

When the tiny Bogues first joined the league, sportswriters had a field day, labeling him, among other things, tiny, pint-sized, dwarflike, bantam, and minute.

But it wasn't always that way. . . .

Tyrone Bogues was born on January 9, 1965, in East Baltimore, Maryland, to Elaine and Richard Bogues. There

In a league where six-foot-six-inch point guards are common, Tyrone "Muggsy" Bogues is an uncommon phenomenon.

was nothing unusual about his height until he reached the ninth grade. Until that time he had been of average height for his age, and as he entered school that year, he stood exactly five feet three inches tall. "Then I stopped growing," he recalls. While his classmates shot up in size, Tyrone Bogues stayed at the same height.

Being short came as no surprise. After all, his mother, Elaine, is herself only four feet eleven inches tall. By comparison, Tyrone towers over her. His father, Richard, was five feet five inches, and Bogues has brothers who are each five feet seven inches tall and a sister who measures five feet one inch in height.

"We're the fives family," says Bogues. "I knew I wasn't going to get out of the five-foot range."

Height was of little concern to Tyrone as he grew up in the tough, poverty-stricken Lafayette Courts housing projects near downtown Baltimore. A cycle of drugs and violence existed there before he was born and penetrated every aspect of the lives of residents. Simply surviving each day without experiencing threats of physical danger was quite an accomplishment that had nothing to do with how tall or short you were. "Inner-city life is harsh," Bogues says today. "Life for us was never easy."

The explosive atmosphere surrounding the Bogues family hit home when Tyrone's father went to prison for armed robbery. Tyrone was only twelve years old at the time.

"I grew up as hard as you can get it," he told Bruce Newman of *Sports Illustrated*. "I wasn't proud of what my pops did, but I guess at the time he felt that was his only means of survival. He used to write me while he was in prison."

The letters he received encouraged Tyrone to work hard in school and continue participation in sports, something the young boy loved. Bogues threw himself into athletic competition with a drive seldom seen on any schoolyard.

Sports became his way of letting off steam, an outlet for his frustrations. Leon Howard, director of the Lafayette Court Recreation Center in Baltimore, remembers that young Tyrone was an aggressive participant in the center's annual summer camps. "He walked like a peacock," Howard said. "He always had his head up, and he walked with a little strut. He wasn't afraid of anybody." Howard also recalled that Bogues wanted to be out in front, leading the pack. Every morning, he insisted on carrying the flag while the rest of the campers recited the Pledge of Allegiance. "I remember him so well walking out with the flag in his left hand and his right hand over his heart," said Howard.

However, his fellow campers are more apt to remember young Tyrone as a bulldog on the ballfields and basketball courts. One of them, Dwayne Wood, casually remarked to Howard that Tyrone was "out there, mugging everybody" in football and basketball games. Pretty soon, everybody in the neighborhood was calling him "Muggsy." He didn't like the nickname at first, but it would stay with him forever.

Muggsy would not forget Dwayne Wood, either.

Dwayne went on to star at Baltimore's Dunbar High School, Maryland's premier basketball school. What attracted Muggsy to Dwayne Wood was the fact that Dwayne, at five feet five inches, stood only two inches taller than Muggsy. Dwayne eventually went on to college stardom as a point guard at Virginia Tech.

"When I was a kid," Bogues said, "my inspiration was Dwayne Wood. He was the guy who made me realize I could play with anybody no matter what my size."

Muggsy bugged Dwayne to play him one-on-one, and the older boy eventually agreed. Soon, the two were playing ball

As a child, Bogues used sports as an outlet for his frustration.

together on playgrounds throughout the neighborhood. Muggsy worshipped Dwyane, but by this time Muggsy was gaining a reputation for himself. Muggsy had become a name of respect and leadership in the Lafayette Court housing projects. "I might have been the smallest kid around," he says, "but I was always in charge."

Establishing a relationship with his two older brothers proved to be difficult. ("They'd get annoyed and tell me to get lost.") It was not surprising, therefore, that he became closer to his sister Sherron. Muggsy was the youngest family member and Sherron was closest to his age. In addition, she was an accomplished basketball player for the Dunbar High School girls' team.

Muggsy recalls Sherron as quick on her feet, a player who didn't hesitate to push the ball up the court. Run-and-gun was her natural style of basketball. An all-star in high school, Sherron was elected to the Dunbar High School Hall of Fame after graduation.

Seeing Sherron's success inspired Muggsy, who set for himself the goal of getting into a good high school like Dunbar. He also realized that basketball would be his ticket to enter the school. Having a famous sister like Sherron wouldn't hurt, either.

Dunbar High School in Baltimore was named for Paul Lawrence Dunbar, a nineteenth-century African-American poet. Dunbar sports teams are nicknamed the Poets. Dunbar is located directly across the street from the Lafayette projects, but for Muggsy in his sophomore year of high school, it might as well have been a thousand miles away.

Somehow Muggsy's academic records from junior high school were misplaced by school officials. As a result, he was unable to transfer to Dunbar. His academic year would be spent at Southern High School, an institution with a reputation for inferior basketball teams. In addition, Southern was located miles from Bogues's home. The school he desperately wanted to go to was just across the street, but now he had to ride not one, but two city buses to attend a school he hated. It took an hour each way to travel to and from the school. Muggsy was so downhearted that he forgot to stay focused on basketball, the thing that meant the most to him. Confused and hurt, he dropped out of the Southern High basketball autumn conditioning program.

To Muggsy, it seemed that the world had turned against him. Fortunately, he kept up with his schoolwork, but basketball just wasn't the same anymore. Yet, he expected to easily make the varsity team when basketball season rolled around that November.

He had not been giving full effort in team workouts, and it showed. One day, Southern High coach Meredith Smith lined the players up and announced the names of the top twenty who could try out for the varsity team. Muggsy's name, however, was not included on the list. Stunned, Bogues boarded his city bus that evening. As he rode along, he pledged to renew his interest in the sport he loved. He would go to Leon Howard and ask to play recreation league ball that winter.

"Mr. Howard," Muggsy recalls, "got me into the fourteen-to-sixteen-year-old leagues to keep my skills sharp." Leon Howard is one of those little-known heroes of American life who is responsible for saving more lives than even he can comprehend. His "rec" leagues provided a place to go for troubled youngsters with time on their hands, time that otherwise might be spent on the dangerous streets of the inner city.

Meanwhile, the Southern varsity basketball team had lost six of its first seven games. Coach Smith asked Muggsy if he was interested in trying out for the team. Confused, Muggsy went to Leon Howard for advice. Howard advised him to give it a try.

Muggsy made the team and eventually became a starter. In a game against Lake Clifton High School, Southern was trailing by five points late in the contest. Muggsy stole the ball and passed to a teammate. The teammate scored easily. Lake Clifton advanced the ball only to have Muggsy steal it again and pass to a teammate who drove in for a layup. With 20 seconds left in the game, Southern was down by only one point. Again, Muggsy stole the ball and passed to a teammate who glided toward the basket for an uncontested layup. Unfortunately, the ball rolled off the rim and Southern lost. The rest of the season resembled that game, with Muggsy

After finally making the Southern varsity basketball team, Muggsy Bogues became a starter.

starring and the team battling but falling just short of victory. What was worse for Muggsy was the knowledge that some of his best playground friends were starring for Dunbar, kids like Reggie Williams and Reggie Lewis. (The trio of Williams, Lewis, and Bogues would later make the National Basketball Association.) Muggsy would eventually have two years of competition at Dunbar High, and what a pair of years they were.

"Muggsy was well-known," said Williams. "The fans loved to come to our games and watch him play. Everyone respected him." Bob Wade, Dunbar's coach and later coach at the University of Maryland, said that during the seasons of 1981–1982 and 1982–1983 the Dunbar basketball court became "Muggsy's world" where "people had to play within his rules and guidelines."

Bogues recalls that during this period, he "didn't follow the NBA all that much. I was mainly involved with the guys around the neighborhood. I didn't have NBA heroes because I couldn't really relate to them. I had neighborhood heroes."

And what heroes they were. Reggie Williams was a certified high school superstar at Dunbar and Muggsy Bogues's best friend there. In one game, Muggsy drove into the lane and performed a 360-degree spin move, flipping the ball behind his neck to Williams, who executed a slam dunk. No one there had ever seen anything like it.

Reggie Lewis was a quiet kid who matured later than his teammates. He eventually became a force to be reckoned with in Maryland high school basketball before going on to star with Northeastern University and the Boston Celtics. Sadly, he died of heart failure in 1993.

As the result of an undefeated season, Dunbar High was ranked No. 1 in the nation by *Basketball Weekly* before the 1982–83 season began. Many teams have folded under such pressure, especially on the high school level. But not Dunbar.

The team enjoyed another undefeated season, including a 120–49 win over Muggsy's old Southern High team.

"The legend of Muggsy Bogues," wrote sportswriter Bob Ryan, "began back in Baltimore, where Dunbar High was kicking butts with a team featuring Reggie Williams and Reggie Lewis." Ryan pointed out that Bogues was elected the Poets' most valuable player and earned for himself the nickname, the Human Assist.

Others carried the scoring load, but it was Muggsy Bogues who dished them the passes that set up their baskets. He ran the Dunbar offense as though he was the team's coach, calling out plays, positioning players, and feeding the open man. Defensively, he picked opponents' pockets, swiping the ball so rapidly they often didn't even realize it was gone.

One game in particular stands out. The Poets were playing Camden (New Jersey) High School. At stake was the No. 1 high school rating in the United States. Camden featured three future University of Louisville stars: Billy Thompson, Milt Wagner, and Kevin Walls. "All of the Camden starters went over to Tyrone before the center jump," recalls Coach Wade. The Camden players were laughing, pointing, and joking over which one would get to guard "the little kid."

Wade remembers that Muggsy walked over to him and said, "Coach, don't worry about a thing." Muggsy Bogues then outplayed Thompson, Wagner, and Walls. "We won by 25 points," Wade said. Muggsy held Walls to 9 points and stole the ball from him 7 times, including three times in a row.

Chapter 3

John Thompson is one of basketball's biggest living legends. From playing in the NBA as a six-foot-ten-inch center with the world champion Boston Celtics to a coaching career that has included NCAA and United States Olympic competition, Thompson has towered over his peers in the profession. In the Baltimore-Washington, D.C., area, Thompson, Georgetown University's basketball coach, maintains an all-powerful presence over the area's athletes.

When Bogues's best friend at Dunbar High School, Reggie Williams, was actively recruited early on in his senior season by Thompson, it was a great honor. Another Dunbar star from Muggsy's junior year, David Wingate, had also been recruited by Thompson and was playing as a freshman for the Georgetown Hoyas. First Wingate, then Williams. Bogues hoped he would be next. Playing for Georgetown would help him to realize all of his dreams, he thought.

He knew, however, that the odds were against a five-foot-three-inch guard going to Georgetown, no matter how good he was on the floor. So it was no surprise when he heard that Thompson really wasn't interested in recruiting him. "Coach Thompson was honest enough with Coach Wade to admit that I wouldn't play much for him," Bogues said.

In reality, few Division I college basketball programs were willing to give an athletic scholarship to someone so short. The talent scouts passed right by Bogues when they visited Dunbar. Some Division II and Division III colleges were willing to give him a try, but that wasn't good enough for Muggsy Bogues. Didn't they know he was Dunbar's most valuable player?

One Division I coach was willing to look past Bogues's height and watch closely to see what he could actually accomplish on the basketball floor. That coach was Carl Tacy of Wake Forest University in Winston-Salem, North Carolina. Through his assistant coach, Ernie Nestor, he put out the word to Coach Wade that a full basketball scholarship might be possible for Bogues, regardless of his height—or lack of it.

Wake Forest University coach Carl Tacy was able to look past Bogues's lack of height in order to recognize his incredible talent.

Bogues prayed that Coach Tacy would come through with a Wake Forest scholarship.

At Winston-Salem, the school's fans and alumni were openly amused when they read of Tacy's interest in a "midget" guard. Wake Forest belongs to the prestigious Atlantic Coast Conference (ACC), but seldom is remembered among other big-name conference schools such as Duke, North Carolina, Maryland, Georgia Tech, Virginia, and North Carolina State. Every major college conference has a Wake Forest in its lineup: a small private university with high academic standards that annually struggles to keep up with publicly-financed members.

In athletics, Wake Forest had been an ACC unknown until a former NBA star named Horace "Bones" McKinney coached the team to a Final Four NCAA tournament appearance in 1962. However, the team had little success after that. When Carl Tacy took over as head coach in 1973, he inherited a team that had won only eight out of twenty-six games under former coach Jack McCloskey. Tacy's teams didn't start winning until 1976, but they kept it up from then on. His Wake Forest team had made a 1977 trip to the NCAA Midwest Regional finals, where they lost to eventual champion Marquette, and had made three straight subsequent appearances in postseason play.

Expectations were high among the fans in Winston-Salem, and those hopes didn't include a five-foot-three-inch point guard. But a patient Tacy was recruiting Muggsy Bogues on the basis of his ability, not his size. He offered Bogues a full scholarship to attend Wake Forest. Bogues indicated he felt honored to accept it.

Upon arriving in Winston-Salem, Bogues knew he was a fish out of water. This was the South; moreover, it was the Old South. Wake Forest University was founded in northern

Wake County, North Carolina, on ground formerly occupied by the Calvin Jones Plantation. But Bogues didn't have to worry about attending a university located on grounds formerly occupied by a slave-owning plantation master. In 1956, Wake Forest University had been relocated to a beautiful 320-acre site northwest of Winston-Salem. The move did little to change the school's reputation as America's foremost Southern Baptist institution of higher learning. Its graduates have included U.S. Senator Jesse Helms, golf great Arnold Palmer, and football player Brian Piccolo.

"Wake Forest's colors," wrote author Steve Holstrom in his book *The ACC Companion*, "can be traced to 1895 when the school adopted a tiger's head in old gold and black as its symbol." While the gold and black stayed as the school colors, the tiger did not. Nicknames were the "Old Gold and Black" and "The Baptists." In 1922, the school newspaper wanted a more "devilish" symbol to represent the fighting

As an African-American student attending an Old South school, Muggsy Bogues felt like a fish out of water.

spirit of the Wake Forest teams. Writer Mayon Parker began using the nickname "Demon Deacons" in all of his sports stories. Wake Forest picked up the name and soon newspapers across the country began using the name." To this day, the school's athletic teams are referred to as "Demon Deacons."

"My first weeks in Winston-Salem were very difficult," Bogues said. "Culture shock is an understatement. Here was a little kid who hasn't been much of anywhere, who has never been on his own, now left alone in . . . what to me was a hick town."

He also felt rejected by Wake Forest teammates who at first assumed that because he was so small, he didn't belong on a major college basketball court. As it turned out, the basketball court became the friendliest place on earth when his teammates saw his sharp, savvy style of play. After that, size differences meant nothing.

Bogues later told *Charlotte Observer* staff writer Charles Chandler that the "toughest year of his life" was his freshman season at Wake Forest. During the basketball season, he was averaging ten minutes of playing time per game, but away from the game, things were tough. "Away from home for the first time, he had trouble adjusting academically and socially. He almost quit," Chandler wrote. One thing kept him at Wake Forest: "I didn't want to go home and see disappointment on my mom's face."

Chapter 4

Carl Tacy, the Wake Forest basketball coach, proved to be a different man in Winston-Salem than the one Bogues had met on recruiting visits. The once-friendly coach had turned out to be more remote, more isolated from his players than Bogues had expected him to be. During his freshman year, Bogues went all out in practice sessions, hustling at both ends of the floor to impress his coach, but his playing time in games was reduced as the season wore on.

The Wake Forest Demon Deacons had one of their best seasons in 1983–84, advancing to the NCAA tournament where they defeated Kansas and DePaul. But when they played Hakeem Olajuwon and the Houston Cougars, Tacy kept Bogues on the bench for all but two minutes of the contest, which the Deacons lost 68–63. To add to Bogues's misery at Wake Forest, an ever-increasing load of classroom work piled up on him while the team was in the tournament. A misunderstanding over a make-up history test resulted in

During his freshman year at Wake Forest, Muggsy Bogues would see his playing time reduced as the season went on.

Bogues's appearance before the school's honor council. Eventually the dean's office was called in to the matter. Bogues had been accused of cheating on the test, but the dean's office cleared him of all charges.

The experience taught Bogues that, academically, athletes were "marked men" on campus, not exactly a comforting thought. Then there was his relationship with Coach Tacy. Would the coach give him more playing time in his sophomore season? The unpredictable coach surprised Wake Forest and the rest of the ACC with the announcement that Muggsy Bogues would be the starting point guard and leader of the Demon Deacons for the 1984–85 season.

The coach's confidence was all Bogues needed. He accepted the challenge handed him and set out to prove his doubters wrong. They didn't have to wait any longer than Wake Forest's first meeting that season with famed ACC powerhouse Duke. Bogues scored 12 points, had 4 steals, and was given credit for 7 assists in the Deacons' 91–89 overtime victory. As the result of that game, he was named ACC Player of the Week. Bogues's big talent was finally recognized.

The victory over Duke turned out to be the highlight of the year for the Wake Forest men's basketball team. The team struggled to a 15–14 record that included an appearance in the National Invitational Tournament. Unfortunately, the Deacons lost in the first round to South Florida, 77–66.

That season, Bogues led the team in assists with 207 and steals with 85, a Wake Forest record. His shooting percentage was exactly 50 percent, meaning half of the shots he took from the field went in.

But it was stealing the basketball that made Muggsy Bogues famous. Bogues's size and build kept him close to the floor, with a low center of gravity. Instead of viewing his small stature as an obstacle, Bogues turned it into an

Pressuring opponents is one of the things Muggsy Bogues does best.

advantage. His ability to crouch down while playing defense, making himself even smaller, and slap the ball away from taller opponents gave him an edge over taller players. He also had the quickest pair of hands seen anywhere.

"To swipe the ball with frequency takes a rare blend of attributes: timing, guile, intelligence, and anticipation," observed *Sports Illustrated* writer Hank Hersch. Bogues's quickness and instincts, combined with his dedication to playing "in your face" defense, created problems for many of Wake Forest's opponents. "Bogues will dominate the ground space, disrupting dribbles, and heading off chest passes," Hersch wrote. "He'll thread, shred, and inspire dread."

Intensity is the key, according to Bogues. "I play each possession like it's the last one of the game. I'm always trying to get a steal. I'm always pressuring my opponent, trying to throw him off rhythm. That's where I generate all my energy, trying to cause my opponent problems and hope that he gets distracted."

Indeed, it was a Bogues steal against Duke in overtime that had sealed the Deacons' victory in that first game. Duke was advancing on a fast break when Bogues caught the break leader from behind, knocked the ball loose, and retrieved it before it went out of bounds.

After his sophomore season, Bogues went home to visit some of his old Dunbar teammates in Baltimore. After an exhibition game on the Dunbar court, he was introduced to a young woman named Kim Lee, whose uncle was a member of the Poets booster club. According to Bogues, it was love at first sight for both. The two began dating and eventually married.

Bogues had a lot on his mind that summer, not the least of which was a surprise announcement by Coach Tacy that he was resigning as Wake Forest head coach. The news shocked the team. Uncertainty followed. All of the returning members of the team had been recruited by Tacy, who had promised them he would be their coach throughout their college careers. One player, Kenny Green, announced he was leaving school to enter the NBA draft.

Three veteran starting players, Muggsy Bogues, Charlie Thomas, and Mark Cline, decided to return for the next season, but the question remained—who would be their coach?

The collegiate basketball world was shocked when Wake Forest announced that Bob Staak of Xavier University would take over for Tacy. Most observers felt that Gary Williams, then at Boston College, was certain to be the next coach.

Muggsy Bogues was one of the first people Staak met with after arriving on campus. He told Bogues that he expected him to lead the team in Bogues's remaining two years at Wake Forest. Coach Staak liked a run-and-gun racehorse-style of basketball, and that suited Bogues fine. The coach also wanted Bogues to be his scoring leader as well as top man in assists and steals, a heavy responsibility. He also told Bogues that he would be co-captain that season, along with Cline.

From the time he realized that he wouldn't grow up to be as tall as Wilt Chamberlain, Muggsy Bogues had fought hard and welcomed new challenges. This would be his biggest challenge, and he welcomed it, too.

To say Bogues set the world on fire in his junior year at Wake Forest would be incorrect. Despite an up-tempo offense and pressure defense, the team limped to an 8-win, 21-loss record. Worse, all eight wins were against non-conference opponents. The Deacons went winless in the Atlantic Coast Conference.

Wake Forest alumni and fans were disappointed in their new coach. About the only positive aspect of a season full of negatives was the star-quality play of Muggsy Bogues. For the second consecutive year, he led the conference in assists and steals. He also scored an average of 11.3 points per game. More significantly, he set the all-time Wake Forest record for steals with 89 in one season. In a game against North Carolina in 1986, he set an all-time Wake Forest record for assists in a single game with 17.

The National Basketball Association began to take an interest in the number of assists this five-foot-three-inch player was accumulating in his college career. In the NBA, almost any player can score, but what is really appreciated are players who can set up the scorers. This is an art that few can practice without flaw. Scouts began to discount Bogues's height and pay more attention to his impressive assist totals.

To his surprise, Bogues was invited to try out for a position on the United States team that would compete that summer for the World Basketball Championship in Spain. After a grueling three weeks of practice, Bogues was told by Coach Lute Olson of Arizona State University that he had made the team. The international exposure that Bogues received as a result of the World games opened even more NBA eyes as the United States team defeated Russia in the finals, 87–85.

That summer, Bogues became a celebrity in European basketball circles. Reporters followed him wherever he went. His short stature and frenzied play during the tournament prompted Pedro Luis Gomez of the *El País* newspaper to write: "He is spectacular to see. He has nerves of steel and super-flexible muscles. On the court he appears to be a little brother of his teammates; but it is he who orders, commands, and directs the action."

Back at Wake Forest, there was other good news. The Demon Deacons had been recognizing a Most Valuable Player since 1957 when the trio of Jack Murdock, Jack Williams, and Ernie Wiggins shared the award. The Wake Forest MVP award was named for Murray Greason, the

Deacons' coach with the most wins. In 1986, the announcement came from the Wake Forest sports information department that the newest Greason Award winner would be point guard Tyrone "Muggsy" Bogues.

Nearly overwhelmed with the sudden attention he received, Bogues paused to remind his friends, fans, and relatives that he still had one year of competition left at Wake Forest. He promised to make it his best ever. Recognizing this, Coach Staak once again made him the Deacons' co-captain with Mark Cline.

"It's hard to believe that [5'3"] Tyrone Bogues is a senior," wrote Smith Barrier, former president of the U.S. Basketball Writers Association, "still looking like a high school kid, but he's the backbone of the Deacons."

Before the season began, the *Charlotte Observer* polled all of the ACC players and determined that Bogues was the "most respected" player in the conference. If the NBA scouts had failed to recognize him before, that poll, taken of members of

Though Bogues was upset by Coach Tacy's resignation, he found that his new coach, Bob Staack (left), had confidence in him.

college basketball's toughest league, attracted their attention. Bogues's final college season was followed closely.

The Demon Deacons opened the season at home against Coastal Carolina and waltzed to an 80–55 victory, an omen that this year would be better than the last. Victories over Davidson, Baptist, and North Carolina-Wilmington followed. Wake Forest was 4–0 before traveling to Virginia Tech and losing 76–68.

Bogues was determined not only to play his intense game on both offense and defense, but also to have fun in his senior year. The team eventually lost more than it won, but Bogues was having the time of his life.

On January 10, 1987, at home against Clemson University, Bogues tied his record of 17 assists and poured in 23 points in a 91–88 overtime loss. The game was typical of the season Wake Forest would have—spectacular performances by Bogues, great teamwork by his fellow Deacons, and, too often, last-second heartbreaking losses.

Wake Forest finished the year with 14 wins and 15 losses, a record not quite good enough to be invited to the National Invitational Tournament. In his last game as a Demon Deacon, fittingly a 77–73 double-overtime loss to North Carolina State, Bogues had seen to it that his name was permanently written into the Wake Forest record books. He led the team in scoring with 14.8 points per game. His 276 assists (9.5 per game) that season is a record that probably will never be broken by another Deacon. He also led the team in steals with 70. He was the all-time career Wake Forest leader in assists (781) and steals (275). He led the ACC in assists and minutes played for three straight seasons. In addition, he was the all-time ACC leader in assists and steals.

One statistic continues to still amaze the experts. After his final season at Wake Forest, it was determined that Bogues averaged 3.8 rebounds per game to rank second among all the guards in the ACC. That's nearly four rebounds per game for a man who stands only five feet three inches tall! No wonder the fans in North Carolina were calling him Superman.

And, yes, for the second straight year, he was named winner of the Greason MVP award. But the MVP award was nearly forgotten with the subsequent announcement that Bogues had made first-team all-Atlantic Coast Conference.

The highest honor, however, came when the athletic department at Wake Forest announced that the basketball team was retiring Bogues's number, fourteen. No Demon Deacon basketball player would be allowed to wear that number again. It is held on permanent reserve on the Wake Forest basketball floor in honor of Bogues's many accomplishments.

Though he won Wake Forest's MVP award in both his junior and senior seasons, Muggsy Bogues's last game as a Deacon was a disappointing loss against North Carolina State.

Chapter 5

The Washington Bullets drafted Tyrone "Muggsy" Bogues as the twelfth collegiate player selected in the 1987 NBA draft. The draft was unusual in that three members of the 1983 Baltimore Dunbar High School senior class were selected in the first round. Bogues went to Washington, Reggie Williams to the Los Angeles Clippers, and Reggie Lewis to the Boston Celtics. It soon became apparent that the Bullets drafted Bogues because of his ability as a point guard, his popularity as a local hero from nearby Baltimore, and his size, which made him a box office attraction. He would become the smallest player in the history of the NBA.

Unfortunately, the last two reasons had the most to do with Washington's decision to draft Bogues. Every NBA team exists to make money for its owners. Usually, the more fans that pay admission to games, the more money a team makes. The Bullets had in mind a number of promotions featuring the popular Bogues and felt his presence on their roster would gain them international attention. "When the Bullets drafted me," Bogues said, "I believed that they were really committed to me. However, I soon realized I was a novelty act. I was just being used to sell tickets."

Novelty act or not, Bogues used the money from his first professional contract to buy his mother a new house away from the Lafayette Courts housing projects. He also went to work on getting his father out of prison.

There was no doubt that Bogues had the talent to be in the league. "What he doesn't have in length," said then-Los Angeles Lakers coach Pat Riley, "he has in quickness, strength, legs, drive, jumping ability, timing, and shooting."

The Bullets, however, apparently saw him as a smaller version of Red Klotz, a five-foot-seven-inch guard for the old Baltimore Bullets. Klotz eventually wound up as a professional basketball clown playing in rigged games against the Harlem Globetrotters. When comparisons were made between the two, Bogues could only shrug his shoulders and say, "My height is going to be talked about, it's going to be used. I've just got to accept that." His playing time dwindled as the season wore on. "When I got to the NBA," he recalls, "I was a curiosity."

According to Fran Blinebury of the *Houston Chronicle*, "Fans in airports and shopping malls and out on the streets were coming up and measuring themselves against this mighty mite and then wondering how in the world he does it." Often they would pat him on the head. Bogues had become something he dreaded—the Washington Bullets mascot. A security guard once refused Bogues entrance into the team's locker room because he mistook him for a child.

Another aspect of Bogues's life was working out better. His efforts to obtain an early release from prison for his father were now beginning to show positive results. A friend had recommended a top attorney to Bogues, and the attorney was able to help get his father paroled. Richard Bogues was able to see his son play basketball in person for the first time. Unhappily, Bogues spent a good deal of that game on the bench.

"I think the coaching staff started second-guessing themselves about the decision that they made to draft me," Bogues said. "They got caught up in listening to other people." What these people were saying was that a five-foot-three-inch point guard could not possibly be an NBA starter. So, Bogues remained on the bench.

It was nice to be near his hometown of Baltimore, but his situation in the NBA was, as he said, "uncomfortable." He began to doubt his abilities. "I was unhappy," he said. "I wasn't playing. It wasn't a good situation." To this day, he believes the Bullets gave up on him too quickly. "For them to give up on a number one pick that early, it was kind of unusual." A big problem involved the Bullets' new coach Wes Unseld. Bogues's previous coaches, Wade, Tacy, and Staak, had been like second fathers to him. Unseld was more distant.

The season dragged on, and it became apparent that, with an expansion draft on the horizon, Bogues would not be protected by the Bullets. This did not necessarily bother him because he wanted to get away and get a fresh start with one of the NBA's new expansion teams, Miami or Charlotte.

Bogues finished the 1987–88 season averaging only 5 points per game with 404 assists and 127 steals. The Bullets, as predicted, left him open to the expansion draft and, on June 23, 1988, he was selected by the Charlotte Hornets. He was going back to North Carolina where, with Wake Forest, he had been the most respected player in the Atlantic Coast Conference.

Once a textile-milling town, Charlotte had blossomed in the late 1980s into the third-largest financial center in the

After getting very little playing time as a rookie in Washington, Bogues
was selected in the expansion draft by the Charlotte Hornets.

United States. While the city sprawled outward in an unprecedented period of population growth, the buildings in the old central business district were being replaced by glittering new structures. Long overlooked by major league sports, the city was more than ready to welcome the Hornets, one of the two newest members of the National Basketball Association. Charlotte seemed to Bogues to be vibrant, alive, and pulsating with action. Here was the ideal place for a second chance.

But as Bruce Newman of *Sports Illustrated* reported, "Dick Harter, who was Charlotte's first coach, had no more faith in Bogues than the Bullets had." Bogues and Harter never hit it off. Once, while describing Bogues's style of play to reporters, Harter fell to his knees to demonstrate how Bogues matched up with center Patrick Ewing of the New York Knicks. "Will a midget really bother Ewing?" Harter asked. "Try shooting over a building when you're only [5′3″."]

This was to be Bogues's most difficult season. He firmly believed he had been handed the opportunity to show the NBA that he could play with the best of them on a new team in a new city that was eager to see him participate. Regrettably for Bogues, Harter did not feel the same way.

The NBA record books show that Bogues's second year in the league matched his first. He averaged only slightly more than five points per game. His number of assists increased, but his number of steals decreased. His playing time (1,755 minutes in 79 games) was only slightly more than it was with Washington. The team itself was dreadful, losing 62 of 82 games.

But George Shinn, owner of the Hornets, had the power to make changes for the Hornets—and for Bogues. Shinn is a native of Kannapolis, North Carolina. He worked in a textile mill, washed cars, and was a janitor in a school he would later own. From this school, the Rutledge Education system grew, and a chain of schools became the building blocks of the Shinn fortune. He eventually expanded his horizons and now owns a real estate development company, auto dealerships, a publishing house, a traffic reporting company, and the Charlotte Hornets NBA franchise.

A lifelong sports fan, Shinn openly credits his accomplishments to a positive attitude, good people, and faith. Shinn easily recognizes positive attitudes among his employees; he quickly saw that quality in Muggsy Bogues. One by one, he questioned Hornets' players about their coach. When Bogues was approached, he replied that he and the coach would be better off parted. One of them should go.

On January 31, 1990, assistant coach Gene Littles replaced Harter. Under the new coach, Bogues was installed as Charlotte's starting point guard, and his life changed. Littles turned Bogues loose to run the team as he saw fit and act as the Hornets' coach on the floor. Muggsy Bogues took the opportunity and ran with it. Soon, sportswriters around the league took notice of him.

"Of all the amazing natural phenomena in the NBA, and there are plenty, nothing is as astonishing as the sight of Tyrone 'Muggsy' Bogues," wrote Bob Ryan in *Sport* magazine. "He is the very symbol of guts, since, superbly muscled little athlete that he is, he is going to be running into picks set by huge hunks of flesh and sinew. He can only survive by putting that little body on the line, and he is more than willing to do it."

Survival was of primary importance in that second Charlotte Hornets' season. Bogues's teammates were of average ability. If each of them could have packaged Muggsy's talent, desire, and guts into their own, larger bodies, the team would never have lost a game. As it was, the luckless Hornets lost 63 games, but ended the second season with the seventy-first consecutive sellout at the Charlotte Coliseum. In typical fashion, however, the Hornets lost the season finale to Dallas, 111–102.

Bogues's fourth NBA season (and Charlotte's third) was marked by some improvement, but not much. "As a group," wrote Mark Engel in *Street & Smith's Pro Basketball Annual*, "the Charlotte Hornets play a scrappy brand of defense, but they are pretty weak when they have the basketball."

Chuck Daly, coach of the Detroit Pistons, was sympathetic. "The Charlotte Hornets have great fan support [every game continued to be sold out]. They show you what NBA basketball is all about. Their club plays hard and usually is in the game until the last five minutes." Those last five minutes are known in the NBA as "crunch time," when the cream rises to the top. Unfortunately for the Hornets, they had only one premier crunch-time player, Muggsy Bogues. Once again, he led the team in assists and steals, but, quite

Though Muggsy Bogues's talent was undeniable, the Charlotte Hornets were still not able to accomplish anything substantial during their first three years as an NBA team.

simply, he could never be the scoring and rebounding leader his team desperately needed.

Things changed forever for the Charlotte Hornets on June 26, 1991, when the team drafted forward Larry Johnson of the University of Nevada at Las Vegas. "There are guys who can talk and there are guys who can play basketball," wrote Fran Blinebury of the *Houston Chronicle*. "Then there are guys like Larry Johnson who can do both things at once."

After Johnson played his first exhibition game, Michael Jordan of the Chicago Bulls remarked, "He's aggressive and plays with a lot of confidence, like he's been in the league a long time. He's going to be in the top five percent of NBA players." Johnson met every expectation, winning the Rookie of the Year award—instantly becoming Charlotte's top scorer and rebounder. Even so, the team could manage only 31 wins in Johnson's first season.

In addition to Johnson, Charlotte also had a new coach, Allan Bristow. A former star NBA player with the San Antonio Spurs, he had previously served as the team's vice president of basketball operations. Bristow completed his second season as coach by leading the Hornets to their first winning season and playoff appearance in team history. A key ingredient in the Hornets' success was Georgetown University's Alonzo Mourning, who was selected by Charlotte in the first round of the 1992 NBA draft that June. The six-foot-ten-inch Mourning played center and finished second on the team and second among all NBA rookies in scoring and rebounding.

Fans suspected things would be different in Charlotte that season when the team finished November with a 7–6 win-loss record. This was only the fourth winning month in the team's history. Bogues paced the team in assists with more than 9 per game, which placed him among league leaders. Charlotte was 7–7 in December and their record stood at 14–13, their best start in the team's history. No longer could they be ranked with the NBA's also-rans. Bogues continued to be the team's floor leader, averaging 12 points and 10.4 assists.

A 117–107 win over the Detroit Pistons on Valentine's Day, 1993, gave Charlotte 26 wins and 12 losses. The team was finally getting the national respect it deserved, and Bogues was playing his best basketball. The rookie Mourning was leading the team in scoring with 21 points per game. April turned out to be the most successful month in Charlotte history when the team won 9 games and lost only 3. One of the most memorable games was a 104–103 victory over Michael Jordan and the Chicago Bulls as Dell Curry stole an inbounds pass to seal the victory. Charlotte clinched their first-ever playoff spot with a 119–111 win over Milwaukee. Bogues finished the regular season with 711 assists and 161 steals. Plus, he averaged 10 points per game, his best ever.

Charlotte faced the Boston Celtics in the first round of the NBA playoffs and lost the first game, 112–101, before 14,890 spectators at Boston Garden, despite a game-high 15 assists from Bogues. The second game turned out to be a classic NBA playoff struggle. In only its second double-overtime win ever, the Hornets triumphed by a score of 99 to 98. The game featured 17 lead changes and 19 ties. Veteran power forward Kevin McHale led the Celtics with 30 points and 10 rebounds. It was the perennial all-pro McHale's last appearance in Boston Garden. He retired after the series ended. McHale's retirement was symbolic as it marked the end of an era of greatness for the Celtics. But, while Boston was on its way out as an NBA power, the young Hornets were on their way in. This was evidenced by Charlotte sweeping the Celtics in the next two games at the Charlotte Coliseum. The Hornets had won their first-ever playoff series.

Their next playoff opponent was the New York Knicks, another team on the rise. The first game of this series was at Madison Square Garden, and the Knicks breezed to a 111–95 win. Charlotte appeared to be in awe of their surroundings as the team was outscored 31 to 15 in the fourth quarter. In the second game, the Hornets led with six minutes and thirty seconds left in the contest, but could not hold on, falling to New York 105–101 in overtime.

The Hornets were in low spirits as they returned home to the Charlotte Coliseum for the third game in the series. Bogues realized Charlotte needed a lift in the worst way and was determined to produce it. He was the team leader, the one responsible for providing the victory spark and, on April 14, 1993, he delivered. His successful jump shot and two free

After winning their first-ever playoff series against the Boston Celtics, Muggsy Bogues and the Hornets went on to face the New York Knicks.

throws in the final 53 seconds of the second overtime proved to be the difference as the Hornets won a 110–106 decision over the Knicks. Bogues and Mourning combined to score 12 of the Hornets' 16 points in the two overtimes. Bogues was a ball of fire as he recorded 3 of his 5 steals in the second overtime. All in all, the Hornets forced 25 New York turnovers.

New York won the third game, and eventually the series, after Bogues turned the ball over as time expired in a 94–92 Knicks victory. The record books for the 1992–93 season show that Muggsy Bogues led the team in assists (8.8 per game) and steals (2 per game) for his fifth consecutive season. At the end of the season he was ranked fifth in the league and second among Eastern Conference guards in assists. For the sixth consecutive season, he had more than 100 steals. This is pretty good for a player everyone said was too short to make it in the NBA.

Chapter 6

The Charlotte Hornets had to look at the 1993–94 season as a disappointment because numerous injury problems forced the team into reverse gear. Charlotte went backward by not making the playoffs and had to once again prove themselves in the conference. This would be difficult to accomplish because the team had no first-round draft pick. No player the caliber of a Larry Johnson or an Alonzo Mourning would be added to the team to upgrade its talent. The 1994–95 Hornets would be essentially the same team that finished with 41 wins and 41 losses in the previous season.

One footnote to the season appeared in *Sports Illustrated*: "Line of the Week—Muggsy Bogues, Hornets, 18 assists, one turnover, three steals. His assist-to-turnover ratio for the season of 4.5 to 1 is tops in the NBA, but in a 112–108 Charlotte win over Orlando on April 14, the five-foot, three-inch guard outdid even himself. By the way, he also had eight points and three rebounds."

A subsequent *Sports Illustrated* issue brought up another little-known Bogues fact: "At five-feet, three-inches, he will never be considered a shot blocker, but despite giving away eight (or more) inches to opponents, he was able to block at least two shots in each of his first seven NBA seasons." No wonder they called him "Little Big Man."

Unfortunately, Bogues could not turn around a floundering team all by himself. NBA analysts didn't know what to make of Charlotte as the 1994–95 season started. While potent on offense, the team had slipped defensively. Only the Bullets and the Clippers had allowed more points the previous season. Bogues was generally acknowledged as an unequaled defensive talent, but Johnson and Mourning were apt to draw criticism for their frequent defensive lapses. Many critics anticipated that the 1994–95 season could be the start of a long, downhill slide for the Hornets. They could not have been more incorrect.

The season began with the Hornets traveling to Chicago for the opening of the new United Center Arena there. A full house of 22,313 spectators watched as previously unheralded J. J. English sparked an 11–0 run, leading to an 89–83 Bulls victory. Bogues had 6 points, 3 assists, and 2 steals. Things would be different at home, he told his teammates. The "friendly confines" of the Charlotte Coliseum, he said, would help the Hornets defeat the Cleveland Cavaliers in the home opener. It was not to be. Muggsy Bogues geared up his game with 14 points and 10 assists, but once again the Hornets lost, 115–107, before the usual sellout crowd of 23,698 eager Charlotte fans. Orlando arrived in Charlotte on November 9. Shaquille O'Neal had an outstanding game, even by his own high standards, scoring 45 points and hauling down 20 rebounds. The game went into overtime, but the Magic's Nick Anderson scored on a layup with one second left on the clock to give Orlando a 130–128 victory. All of a sudden, the

Hornets were 0–3, and the naysayers in the crowd were already predicting a losing season.

It took only two days for the team to change things. The Hornets journeyed to the Bradley Center in Milwaukee to face the Bucks. Bogues knew he had to elevate his play to help Charlotte break the losing streak. He scored 12 points, dished out 11 assists, and had 2 steals in a 123–115 Hornet victory. The next night, the Hornets returned home to face Detroit. Bogues didn't want to see the team's momentum stalled, and he made up his mind to shoot the ball more than he usually did. The result was 22 points (in addition to 13 assists and 1 steal), and a 113–100 win over the Pistons. Singlehandedly, Bogues had pulled the Hornets out of their slump.

Muggsy Bogues continued his hot play against Indiana at home with 15 points and 12 assists. Up-and-down performances by the team continued through the month of November. Bogues stole the ball six times against the Celtics, but Boston won 98–91. Charlotte did finish the month with a winning record, but only because Larry Johnson put on a show in a 105–95 win over the New York Knicks. Johnson had 23 points, 10 rebounds, and 9 assists, two fewer than Bogues, who had 11.

A five-game road trip began with Denver ambushing the Hornets before 17,171 viewers at McNichols Sports Arena with a 24–9 spurt in the third quarter. Fortunately for the Hornets, the struggling Clippers were next on the schedule, and Charlotte feasted on a 115–93 blowout at the Los Angeles Sports Arena. Charlotte then made 13 three-pointers in an easy victory at Utah. The rigors of the long road trip finally caught up with the Hornets, and they lost at both Houston and Dallas.

Home never looked better to the weary Hornets. They put everything together in a 107–101 victory over the Bucks, with Bogues chipping in 11 assists. The next evening, at Detroit, he led the team in scoring with 18 points in a 106–93 win. He also had 8 assists, 2 steals, and 2 rebounds.

Denver arrived in Charlotte the following night, and the Hornets sailed to a 111–92 victory. Bogues was shooting the ball more than ever and scored 19 points. They next defeated Philadelphia for their third win in a row and five wins out of the last six. Muggsy scored 15 points and recorded 12 assists against the 76ers. A loss to San Antonio broke the streak, but the Hornets resumed their winning ways against Orlando. Bogues was at the top of his game when the Magic came to town. After the dust had cleared, he had scored 18 points, handed out 17 assists, and was credited with 4 steals.

"Bogues has the consummate point-guard mentality," said Dave Twardzik, former NBA player and Hornets' director of player personnel. "That's something we all talk about but very few players have it. He genuinely has it. When you combine that with a tremendous basketball I.Q. and feel for the game, you get a guy who can be a very, very good point guard." The Hornets give Bogues the freedom to race up and down the floor, creating as he moves. He can be deadly when given an open floor.

Bogues scored 17 points and had 11 assists as Milwaukee lost to the Hornets, 101–94. The Hornets would not lose until January 17 when Shaquille O'Neal put on a one-man show with 35 points in a 109–98 Magic romp. By then Charlotte had chalked up 17 wins and 12 losses. Bogues's most spectacular game during the winning streak was against the New Jersey Nets on January 6 when he hit a go-ahead jumper and had a steal and two free throws in the closing seconds as Charlotte came back to edge the Nets, 89–88.

He revealed his secret of success: "I try to visualize what happens before it does," he said. When he has the ball, he noted, each defender will react differently to him. "I have to read every situation," he said. "I have to be aware of the clock and know how to get plays executed. On the floor, I'm thinking all the time, but I feel comfortable with that. It comes naturally." Total concentration on the game has become Muggsy Bogues's hallmark. After all, at only five feet three inches, he has to compensate for his lack of size with intense devotion one hundred percent of the time.

On January 18, the Hornets blew a 22-point lead at home against San Antonio, then Johnson took a perfect pass from Bogues and scored on a layup with fourteen seconds to go for a 111–110 Charlotte victory, their twelfth in a row at home. The assist was one of 15 that Bogues had that night. The Charlotte Coliseum victory streak reached thirteen with a win over the Nets that left the Hornets alone in first place in the Central Division.

Just as things appeared to be operating as smoothly as possible, the Minnesota Timberwolves, with a record of only 9 wins and 29 losses, upset Charlotte, 100–83, at Target Center in Minneapolis. Losses to the Los Angeles Lakers and Atlanta Hawks followed. The red-hot New York Knicks were riding a six-game winning streak when they encountered the reeling Hornets, but Charlotte summoned up the strength to defeat the Knicks easily, 105–90, as Johnson scored a career-high 39 points. Bogues scored 13 and had 12 assists and 2 steals.

Charlotte finished January with 11 wins and only 4 losses, the best month in the franchise's history. Bogues put an exclamation point on the last January victory (over the Bullets) by scoring 20 points. On February 1, his jump shot put the Hornets ahead to stay against the Celtics in a 100–93 Charlotte victory. Two nights later, Bogues burned the nets for 23 points, one short of his NBA career single-game high, in a 117–98 win over the Bucks.

By mid-February, Charlotte had 34 wins and 19 losses,

Bogues tries to visualize what will happen on the court before it actually does. His total concentration has become his hallmark.

including a 100–89 win at home over Sacramento. In that contest, Bogues registered 19 points, 7 assists, and 1 steal. March began with a 109–99 road win over Portland before a sellout crowd of 12,888 at Memorial Coliseum. This was the second game of a long and successful West Coast road trip that saw wins in Phoenix, Seattle, Oakland, and Portland and losses in Los Angeles and Sacramento.

A standing ovation from the always sold-out crowd at the Charlotte Coliseum greeted the Hornets as they returned from the road trip to face the Seattle Supersonics. Once again, the inspired Hornets were led by Bogues, who hit a jump shot to put Charlotte ahead to stay, ending in a 112–99 victory. A home win over Miami followed, but three straight subsequent losses put first place in doubt. The Hornets won their fortieth game at home on March 19 when Bogues and Hersey Hawkins hit crucial free throws in the final sixteen seconds to give Charlotte a 108–104 win over the Utah Jazz. The Hornets then regained first place with a win over the Knicks. Bogues had 12 points and 6 assists.

Losses at Orlando, Philadelphia, and Dallas cost Charlotte first place to the Indiana Pacers. The Hornets recovered with a win on the road against Miami and, on April 5, they defeated Philadelphia, 84–66, in a low-scoring game. The two teams, combined, earned only 19 points in the second quarter. Nonetheless, it was Charlotte's forty-fourth win and matched the team's all-time high for victories. The record for wins was set two nights later when Charlotte beat Washington, 98–93, as Bogues scored 15 points, dished out 8 assists, and had 4 steals.

Indiana dashed any of Charlotte's first-place hopes by crushing the Hornets, 97–68. Pacers' reserves outscored the Hornets' reserves, 25–2, in the first three quarters of the game. Charlotte's forty-sixth win came at home at the expense of the Celtics, 115–95, chalking up the Hornets' eighth victory in the last nine games against the legendary Boston franchise. Bogues had 12 points, 9 assists, and 3 steals against the Celtics.

Although first place had eluded them, Charlotte now looked forward to the playoffs against the Chicago Bulls. A new, and somewhat unexpected, ingredient had been added to the picture. The brilliant all-pro Michael Jordan had returned to basketball after a try at professional baseball and was now leading Chicago in a relentless drive to the playoffs. As luck would have it, their first opponent would be Muggsy Bogues and the Charlotte Hornets. Inadvertently, the schedule-makers had set up a preview of the Hornets-Bulls playoff duel at the United Center in Chicago on April 22. A crowd of 23,544 gathered to see Chicago rip the Hornets, 116–100. However, for the Hornets, the game was more of an exhibition than a postseason preview contest. Charlotte's coach Bristow rested his all-stars— Mourning, Johnson, and Bogues. Jordan, however, did play, and he and Toni Kukoc led Chicago with 19 points each.

To say that Michael Jordan dominated the subsequent playoff series with the Hornets probably is an overstatement; however, he did take center stage, particularly in the opening game. Jordan had been an All-American at North Carolina University and now he was returning to play a playoff opponent in his home state. He celebrated by beating the Hornets, 108–100. Jordan scored 48 points, the thirty-first time in playoff action that he had scored more than 40. Charlotte was able to force the game into overtime, but Jordan hit a bank shot with two minutes left in the extra period to put the game away. Bogues played nearly the entire game and chalked up 10 assists in a losing effort.

Chicago was determined to win both playoff games at the Charlotte Coliseum and raced to a first-half lead in the second game. But the Hornets came roaring back with the teamwork of

Johnson, Mourning, and Bogues. Stung by negative comments about their defensive abilities, the Hornets put the clamps on the Bulls, allowing them to make only 12 of 42 field goal attempts in the second half. Charlotte breezed past Chicago, 106–89, as Bogues scored 13 points and handed out 7 assists.

The next two games in the series would be at the new United Center in Chicago, which had become the Temple of Doom for the Hornets. More than twenty-four thousand yelling, stomping, and whistling fans greeted the Bulls during pregame warmups. When Jordan was introduced by the public address announcer, the crowd nearly tore the building apart. The Charlotte players were so stunned by the avalanche of support for Jordan that they played tentatively. When it was over, the final score read: Bulls 103, Hornets 80. It was the worst playoff loss in Charlotte history. Chicago had taken them on a 19–4 run at the end of the second quarter and never looked back. Jordan scored 25 and Kukoc 22 to lead the Bulls.

Bogues knew that another loss would mean the end of the playoffs for Charlotte. He coaxed, pleaded, and rallied the Hornets out of their Chicago funk for the next game. It almost worked.

Continuing his triumphal return to basketball, the magnificent Jordan scored seven of the Bulls' final nine points. Chicago survived a third-quarter collapse and advanced to the second round of the playoffs by defeating Charlotte by a single point. Bogues and the Hornets had several chances to force a fifth game but could not connect. With eight seconds remaining in the game, Johnson missed a seventeen-foot jump shot. Charlotte grabbed the rebound and called a time-out. Once again, Johnson was passed the ball and he missed a twenty-footer. Flying like an eagle, Hawkins rebounded Johnson's miss and put up a desperation shot that misfired. Curry rebounded Hawkins's miss and put the ball in. But it was too late. Time had run out on the game and the season. As

In the second game of the playoff series against the Chicago Bulls, the teamwork of Muggsy Bogues, Alonzo Mourning, and Larry Johnson led to a 106–89 Charlotte win.

Bulls fans rushed the court, Johnson lay face down near the free-throw circle, unable to believe what had happened.

As for Bogues, he once again led the NBA with a five-to-one assists-to-turnover ratio, but the years of his legs pounding up and down on hardwood floors finally began to catch up with his knees. During the off-season, he underwent surgery on his left knee and missed the first two months of the 1995–96 season.

Without Bogues, the Hornets were like a ship with a missing rudder. *Charlotte Observer* staff writer Rick Bonnell observed that in one particular early-season game, team members "played like they'd never met each other."

Bonnell never would have made that observation if Bogues had been in the game, directing the flow of traffic and creating scoring opportunities.

"People always say we'll probably never see another Larry Bird," said Coach Bristow. "But I've always felt we have a better chance of seeing another Larry Bird than we do another Muggsy Bogues."

Against all odds, Bogues had become an NBA legend.

Because Muggsy Bogues was unable to play due to knee surgery and Alonzo Mourning had been traded to the Miami Heat, the Hornets struggled during the 1995–96 season.

The 1995–96 season saw the Charlotte Hornets at a crossroads in the team's development. Charlotte's brightest star, Alonzo Mourning, turned down a seven-year, $78.4-million contract offer from the Hornets. Team owner George Shinn responded by trading him to Miami, along with LeRon Ellis and Pete Myers, for Glen Rice, Matt Geiger, and Khalid Reeves. Rice, Geiger, and Reeves are NBA players who would be starters for most teams, but none is a superstar comparable to Alonzo Mourning.

After Mourning left, a nine-story mural of Bogues, Mourning, and Johnson on a downtown Charlotte bank building was whitewashed over. The Hornets were seeking a new image. They would do well to seek a new center. The trio of Geiger, ageless Robert Parish, and rookie George Zidek have looked painfully inept when the opposing center was Shaquille O'Neal, Hakeem Olajuwon, Patrick Ewing, Dikembe Mutumbo, or even Andrew Lang.

Reeves was looked upon to replace the injured Bogues, at least temporarily, but floundered in his first several games with the Hornets as opponents routinely altered his shots and stole his passes. The Reeves problem was solved in January by trading him and Kendall Gill for talented point guard Kenny Anderson from the New Jersey Nets. Anderson immediately settled down the backcourt and established himself as the team's leader.

This left Bogues without a starting job when he returned to action in February 1996. Muggsy played sparingly in six games and was put back on the injured list for the rest of the season with a sore left knee, the one that had received arthroscopic surgery. In the six games, he averaged 2.3 points and 3.2 assists. Bogues was also slow to return in the 1996–97 season. Only time will tell how well he will recover from surgery.

Career Statistics

YEAR	TEAM	GP	FG%	REB	AST	STL	BLK	PTS	AVG
1987–88	Washington	79	.390	136	404	127	3	393	5.0
1988–89	Charlotte	79	.426	165	620	111	7	423	5.4
1989–90	Charlotte	81	.491	207	867	166	3	763	9.4
1990–91	Charlotte	81	.460	216	669	137	3	568	7.0
1991–92	Charlotte	82	.472	235	743	170	6	730	8.9
1992–93	Charlotte	81	.453	298	711	161	5	808	10.0
1993–94	Charlotte	77	.471	313	780	133	2	835	10.8
1994–95	Charlotte	78	.477	257	675	103	0	862	11.2
1995–96	Charlotte	6	.375	7	19	2	0	14	2.3
Totals		644	.460	1,834	5,488	1,110	29	5,396	8.4

GP-Games Played   **STL**-Steals
FG%-Field Goal Percentage   **BLK**-Blocks
REB-Rebounds   **PTS**-Points
AST-Assists   **AVG**-Average

Where to Write Muggsy Bogues

Mr. Muggsy Bogues
c/o Charlotte Hornets
One Hive Drive
Charlotte, N.C. 28217

Index

P

Palmer, Arnold, 27
Parish, Robert, 61
Parker, Mayon, 28
Piccolo, Brian, 27

R

Reeves, Kahlid, 61
Rice, Glenn, 61
Riley, Pat, 10, 13, 40
Ryan, Bob, 23, 44

S

Shinn, George, 43, 44, 61
Smith, Meredith, 20
Staak, Bob, 34, 36, 41
Starks, John, 11, 13

T

Tacy, Carl, 25, 26, 29, 31, 33, 34, 36, 41

Thomas, Charlie, 34
Thompson, Billy, 23
Thompson, John, 24
Twardzik, Dave, 53

U

Unseld, Wes, 41

W

Wade, Bob, 22, 23, 25m 41
Wagner, Milt, 23
Walls, Kevin, 23
Wiggins, Ernie, 35
Williams, Gary, 34
Williams, Jack, 35
Williams, Reggie, 22, 23, 24, 39
Wingate, David, 10, 24
Wood, Dwayne, 17, 19

Z

Zidek, George, 61